EXTREME

Lights Out!

Living in 24-Hour Darkness

Sean Callery

Fact Finders is published by Capstone Press,
a Capstone Publishers company.
151 Good Counsel Drive, P.O. Box 669,
Mankato, Minnesota 56002.
www.capstonepress.com

First published 2008

Produced for A & C Black by

Monkey Puzzle Media Ltd
The Rectory, Eyke, Woodbridge
Suffolk IP12 2QW, UK

Library of Congress Cataloging-in-Publication Data

Callery, Sean.
    Lights out! : living in 24-hour darkness / by Sean Callery.
       p. cm. -- (Fact finders. Extreme!)
    Includes bibliographical references and index.
    Summary: "Describes the science behind an arctic
    winter, including its effects on daily life for people and
    wildlife"--Provided by publisher.
    ISBN-13: 978-1-4296-3124-2 (hardcover)
    ISBN-10: 1-4296-3124-4 (hardcover)
    ISBN-13: 978-1-4296-3144-0 (pbk.)
    ISBN-10: 1-4296-3144-9 (pbk.)
    1. Inuit--Arctic regions--Social life and customs--Juvenile
literature. 2. Animals--Arctic regions--Juvenile literature.
3. Cold adaptation--Arctic regions--Juvenile literature. 4.
Arctic regions--Climate--Juvenile literature. 5. Arctic
regions--Social life and customs--Juvenile literature. I.
Title. II. Series.

E99.E7C224 2009
305.897'120719--dc22

2008025077

Editor: Steve Parker
Design: Mayer Media Ltd
Picture research: Lynda Lines
Series consultant: Jane Turner

This book is produced using paper that is made from
wood grown in managed, sustainable forests. It is natural,
renewable, and recyclable. The logging and manufacturing
processes conform to the environmental regulations of
the country of origin.

Printed in China by C & C Offset Printing Co., Ltd

Picture acknowledgements
Alamy pp. 11 bottom (Bryan & Cherry Alexander), 14–15
(Bryan & Cherry Alexander); Bryan & Cherry Alexander
pp. 10, 23; Corbis pp. 22 (Nevada Weir), 28 (Ashley
Cooper); FLPA pp. 11 top (Michio Hoshino/Minden
Pictures), 12 (ZSSD/Minden Pictures); Getty Images pp. 1
(Tom Walker), 8 (David Hiser), 12–13 (Patricio
Robles/Sierra Madre), 17 (Josef Fankhauser), 18–19 (Rex
Ziak), 21 (Duncan McNicol), 26, 27 (Tom Walker), 29
(Steve Bly); iStockphoto pp. 14 left (Gail A. Johnson), 20
(iztoc noc); NASA pp. 5, 25 (JPL); Nature Picture Library
p. 6 (Staffan Widstrand); Photolibrary.com pp. 4 (Doug
Allan/Tartan Dragon), 7 (Ralph Reinhold/ Animals Animals/
Earth Scenes), 15 top (Larry Williams/Flirt/Corbis), 19 right
(Chris Arend/Alaska Stock Images); Science Photo Library
pp. 9 (David Vaughan), 16 (George Holton), 18 inset
(George Steinmetz); Still Pictures p. 24 (Koczy/images.de).

The front cover shows the Aurora Borealis above an
illuminated igloo in Nunavut, Canada (Getty Images/
Wayne R. Bilenduke).

Every effort has been made to contact copyright holders
of material reproduced in this book. Any omissions will be
rectified in subsequent printings if notice is given to the
publishers.

CONTENTS

Abbreviations **s** stands for seconds • **km/h** stands for kilometers per hour • **km** stands for kilometers • **mph** stands for miles per hour • **in** stands for inches • **kg** stands for kilograms • **lb** stands for pounds

Twilight world

We all love the Sun's light and warmth. But the Sun disappears for several months during the Arctic winter. As the light goes out, the Arctic becomes a freezing dark wilderness where food is scarce and life is very tough indeed.

Through August and September, shadows lengthen as the Sun gets lower in the sky. Then it is gone, and the harsh Arctic winter sets in. During the endless night of midwinter, people sleep as much as they can, and find it hard to keep to a routine. Some miss the Sun so much they become depressed.

After the Sun finally sets in late autumn, it won't be back for months.

axis   imaginary line between the North and South Poles

Dark winter

At the North Pole, the Sun disappears on September 24 and returns 179 days later on March 18. At the edge of the Arctic, the Sun goes down on November 18 and rises on January 24, after a darkness of 65 days.

If the Earth wasn't tilted at an angle to the Sun, all places would have the same length of day and night, all year round.

Light travels in straight lines, so it can't reach parts of the planet.

North Pole

The Arctic has long, dark winter nights.

Earth's axis is tilted by 23.5°.

Sun's rays

Earth spins once every 24 hours on its axis.

The Antarctic has long, sunny summer days.

South Pole

Don't move!

How do you get food in a wilderness where no plants grow and the animals see you from miles away and escape? It can be a tough job!

Some hunters wait more than a day near a breathing hole, hoping to shoot a seal.

Imagine staring at a hole in the ice for hours. It's where seals come up to breathe. Your feet feel frozen, but you can't stamp them or make any movement or any sound. That would tell the seal you are there.

Seeing a few bubbles on the surface of the gray water, you raise your gun. The seal's head appears, and you pull the trigger. The seal slumps, and you must leap forward and grab it before it sinks.

Seals are a good source of food. A seal feeds a human family for several days. Nothing is wasted. Its oil can be burned in lamps, and its skin can be made into waterproof boots and clothing.

wilderness large area of wild, empty land

Before guns, hunters jabbed seals with spears or used a harpoon and rope.

Like all **mammals**, seals breathe air, so they have to put their heads above water.

Arctic words

One of the best-known groups of Arctic people are the Inuit, who live in Canada, Greenland, and Alaska.

A seal bites and scratches out several breathing holes in the ice.

mammal warm-blooded, air-breathing animal with fur or hair

Surviving in the freezer

Take off a glove in an Arctic gale, and your hand aches with pain right away. Within minutes the fingers start to freeze solid. Then the only cure is amputation!

Traditional Arctic clothing is made from animal skins and furs.

Heat rises, and our brains must stay warm, so a hat or hood is vital.

Suitable animal furs are seal, reindeer (caribou), polar bear, wolf, and Arctic fox.

Lots of thin layers **insulate** better than one thick coat because they trap warm air between them.

Clothes are sewn using reindeer guts.

Your body works harder in the cold, pumping blood to extremities such as toes and fingers. In freezing conditions, it soon shuts off that supply to protect itself and keep your insides warm. The result is frostbite, as the water in your flesh freezes. Badly frostbitten fingers look black, as if burnt.

Arctic words

Inuit people call soft sealskin boots *kamik*. A hat or hood is *nasak*. A hooded coat is *amautik*.

Average Arctic winter temperatures are about twice as cold as a home freezer. No-one survives for long at -55°F (-48°C) without special protection!

amputation cutting off a body part   **insulate** slow down the movement of heat

Chiller killer

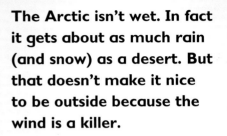

The Arctic isn't wet. In fact it gets about as much rain (and snow) as a desert. But that doesn't make it nice to be outside because the wind is a killer.

*Riding a **snowmobile** with your face or hands exposed is very, very cold!*

Brrr! Cold air attacks your skin.

snowmobile a vehicle with tracks and skis for traveling on snow

With no trees or mountains to stop the Arctic winds, they often blow at 30–80 miles per hour (50–100 kilometers per hour). This makes already low temperatures even colder because moving air feels colder than still air—blow on your arm and see. This effect is called wind chill. An already deadly -31 degrees Fahrenheit (-35 degrees Celsius) feels twice as cold in a gale—or on a speeding snowmobile. People expose as little as possible of their skin to avoid being frostbitten.

Icy winds swirl across the Arctic.

Staying warm

To keep out the cold, Arctic animals have a dense fur coat with long hair and a layer of thick fat under the skin.

Husky sled dogs lie curled nose to tail, to keep out of the wind.

Animals such as musk oxen huddle together to share their heat.

Animals near the middle are protected from the worst of the wind.

Hunters can pick off the animals on the outside.

Make sense of hunting

Predators and prey need all their senses to cope with the Arctic winter. And since few animals could survive hibernation in Arctic temperatures, they must stay awake and continue to hunt.

Under the skin is a 5-in (12-cm) layer of fat for insulation and **buoyancy**.

When polar bear hair gets wet, it sticks together to form a barrier and keep water away from the skin.

Adult polar bears weigh 780–1,320 lb (300–600 kg).

buoyancy staying afloat by an upward force

Small, rounded ears reduce heat loss.

Polar bears emerge from their underground snow dens and use their sense of smell to find prey. Their sensitive nostrils can pick out a walrus—or maybe a human—more than a mile away. Polar bears also have very good hearing. If they detect seals swimming under the sea ice, they smash their paws straight down and grab a tasty treat!

42 very sharp teeth for chomping meat.

Long, sharp claws set in non-slip, padded soles.

Polar bears are carnivorous—they eat mainly meat. They are the only animal that lives on the Arctic ice all year round. Humans are their only predators.

Feet are large to **spread** body weight.

hibernation long winter sleep

A good hiding

Get too close to a walrus or a polar bear, and you'll be ripped apart. Would you have the guts to stalk one?

It isn't completely dark through the Arctic winter. Although the Sun doesn't rise, the moon reflects its light on to the snow to create a silver-gray world. Hunters hide behind white screens to allow them to crawl unseen toward their targets. Then they can either fire a bullet or rush out and surprise their prey.

*Without **camouflage**, people must be very careful with Arctic animals. Hopefully this walrus is tired and will not attack!*

camouflage blending in with the surroundings

White screen hides hunter from prey, which can't see through **opaque** screen.

Kings of the Arctic, polar bears have a natural camouflage screen— their almost-white fur, which blends in with the snow and ice.

Light bounces off pale surface.

LIGHT

opaque material through which light cannot pass

Snow houses

Sometimes hunters need to stay on the ice through the frozen night. A tent isn't warm enough. They must build a snow shelter to survive.

If you can build an igloo, you don't have to fear being trapped on the ice at night. Experienced builders prefer to make them on sea ice, because the sea below is warmer than the deep-frozen land.

Igloos are snow houses made by sloping snow bricks in a **spiral** shape to form a dome. The bricks are cut with a special saw or knife. Once the basic shape is formed, snow is packed into the joints to seal out the wind. Ice is a good insulator and igloos warm up fast once there is a source of heat inside, such as a person or a stove. The heat makes the walls melt and refreeze to form an even stronger barrier.

spiral a circular curve that gets wider and wider, like a snail's shell

Winter shelter, summer tent

Igloos are not permanent houses. They are temporary shelters made during the winter while out hunting. In the warmer summer, hunters use tents made from animal hides. These are cleaned-up animal skins, also used for clothing, blankets, and flooring.

Dome shape is strong and resists being blown down by the wind.

Small entrance is easier to defend against polar bears!

Entrance allows **ventilation** and is low down to stop heat rising up and out.

Most ice blocks fit together snugly to keep out wind.

ilation allowing the passage of air

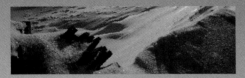

Watch the crack

Ice can be a deadly companion. Recently, a hunter got stuck on an ice floe and drifted for two days. He was rescued, but his legs were frozen solid and had to be cut off.

Arctic travelers walk in single file, to avoid putting too much pressure on thin ice.

Arctic words

Sea ice is far thicker than the freshwater ice of rivers and lakes. Cracks in the ice are called leads.

ice floe sheet of floating ice

If you're out on the ice, check that the wind and water currents are in opposite directions and they balance out. Then any sea ice is less likely to break apart.

Climb a snow ridge or an **iceberg** to see what is ahead.

Snowshoes spread body weight, so they sink less in snow, and ice is less likely to break. They could be a life saver.

Walking across the ice in the dark isn't easy. The wind creates ridges and the ice can change from thick sea ice to thin freshwater ice that bends scarily underfoot. Small cracks can widen so much that they would swallow you. The freezing sea would paralyze you in minutes, with death soon after.

Ice floes can crack apart and float out to sea, maybe carrying a stranded explorer.

iceberg floating lump of ice

Slide show

Trekking across snow is as tough as walking through deep sand—so people slide around the problem!

Arctic hunters take what they need with them—food, clothes, equipment, and fuel. Plus they hope to return with a heavy cargo of animal bodies. They can't carry all this, but a sled on ski-type runners slides easily over ice and snow. Skilled drivers spot thin ice and speed up, to skim across it before the weight of the sled breaks the surface.

*Dog sled racing is a popular sport. The steel runners slide along easily with little **friction**.*

Best friend; meaty meal

Early explorers killed and ate their dogs one by one during the expedition to save carrying too much food.

friction force that opposes motion or slows moving things

Zoom!
Dogs pull the sled at about 10–14 mph (16–22 km/h).

Trouble!
Dogs may jump across the ropes to be near their friends, so the harness and **lines** must be untangled often.

Woof!
Most sled dogs are huskies.

Whoosh!
A speedy sled can cover over 80 miles (130 km) in a day.

Slide!
Dog sleds are the traditional way of traveling around on Arctic ice.

lines leads or ropes with which dogs pull sleds

21

Welcome back!

In the Arctic spring, the Sun's return means a big celebration!

When the Sun rises after winter, people follow an ancient ritual and make half-sad, half-happy faces at the sky. This is to anger the Sun-Woman, who then strikes out at them with rays of light.

Arctic words

Tundra is a treeless, hilly area, possibly named after an old Russian word for "land of no trees." Permafrost is the soil layer just beneath the surface that stays frozen all the time.

Plants that survived the winter as frozen seeds come to life in spring, and the tundra glows with colors.

When the Earth is here, it's summer in the northern **hemisphere**, which faces the Sun.

Seasons are due to the way the Earth goes around the Sun once each year.

Now it's winter in the northern hemisphere ...

It's winter in the southern hemisphere, which is tilted away from the Sun.

Sun

Earth's orbit

... and summer in the southern hemisphere.

The Sun is back! People gather for the first sunrise of spring.

hemisphere northern or southern half of the Earth, divided by the equator

Snow-blind

Inuit people used to wear glasses with a difference—goggles with narrow slits for peeking at the bright summer light.

This eyewear is a sight-saver. Traditional snow goggles were made of bone, wood, or ivory such as walrus tusk.

Sunlight bounces off snow and ice and overloads our eyes, burning the cornea (the front part of the eye). This is snow blindness. It's a big problem in the Arctic when the Sun is low in the sky and reflects off the white all around. A slit only lets a little light through. Today, sunglasses or goggles do the job.

ozone a gas in the atmosphere that absorbs some of the Sun's rays

High up in the atmosphere, the Earth has its "sunglasses." This is a layer of **ozone** gas that filters out the Sun's most harmful cancer-causing rays. However, gases known as **CFCs** have been damaging the ozone layer, creating a hole over each pole. These harmful gases are now banned, and the damage seems to have slowed.

In winter the ozone hole over the Arctic grows larger as wind patterns change.

Colors from red to orange, yellow, and green show where the ozone layer becomes thicker.

Black areas are where the ozone layer is thinnest.

North America

Greenland

Asia

Europe

Friend and enemy

Ozone is our friend high up, blocking harmful solar rays. But when it is low down at street level, we choke on it and struggle to breathe.

In spring the ozone hole over the Arctic shrinks as winds ease off and temperatures rise.

CFCs gases once used in refrigeration and spray cans

Have an ice trip

If you'd like to travel to the Arctic, you're not alone. Every year 1.5 million tourists visit the area.

Arctic visitors can choose from trips to see Santa and his reindeer, cross-country skiing, going on a snowmobile safari to take wildlife photos, and even dogsled racing. They can stay in a hotel made of ice or go cruising on an **icebreaker** ship. A major tourist attraction is the incredible display of lights and colors in the sky, known as the northern lights or Aurora Borealis.

1 The Northern Lights are seen mainly in spring and autumn.

2 The lights are caused by tiny electric particles from the Sun, called the solar wind.

Tourism is big business in the Arctic. These visitors have flown all the way to the North Pole.

icebreaker strong, powerful ship that breaks through ice

3 The particles approach Earth at up to 750 miles/s (1,200 km/s).

4 When the particles hit the Earth's **magnetic** field, their electricity escapes and creates lights in the sky.

Light legends

The northern lights have inspired many stories. Some people thought they were spirits. Others believed they were sparks from the tails of legendary foxes made of fire.

5 The northern lights look like mysterious dancing clouds, constantly changing shape and color.

magnetic attracting iron or steel like a magnet

Melting world

The Arctic is changing. As global warming raises the Earth's temperature, the Arctic world is slowly melting away.

The Inuit way of life has greatly changed. Many Inuit and other Arctic people no longer live as part of nature. They work in the oil business or fish-canning factories, drive transport trucks, or take part in the tourism trade.

The overall area of Arctic ice is now the smallest since records began. The summer sea ice is already disappearing by one-tenth every 10 years. All of this melting ice will raise sea levels around the world, and possibly flood whole cities near coasts.

As this happens, the way of life for Arctic people and animals has to change. Their icy habitat will be smaller, threatening creatures such as polar bears and ice-dwelling seals. It's a giant problem for them and their white world.

global warming general rise in the Earth's temperature

Vast areas of ice reflect some of the Sun's heat (solar radiation) away from Earth.

As ice melts, less heat is reflected. **Climate** change speeds up and global warming worsens.

Disappearing Arctic ice

The Northwest Passage linking the Atlantic and Pacific Oceans is usually blocked with ice. In 2007, ships sailed through fairly easily for the first time.

Glaciers and ice shelves are falling into the sea at an ever-increasing rate.

Extra water from melted ice makes sea levels rise.

climate typical pattern of weather over many years

Glossary

amputation cutting off a body part

axis imaginary line between the North and South Poles

buoyancy staying afloat by an upward force

camouflage blending in with the surroundings

CFCs gases once used in refrigeration and spray cans

climate typical pattern of weather over many years

friction force that opposes motion or slows moving things

global warming general rise in the Earth's temperature

hemisphere northern or southern half of the Earth, divided by the Equator

hibernation long winter sleep

iceberg floating lump of ice

icebreaker strong, powerful ship that breaks through ice

ice floe sheet of floating ice

insulate slow down the movement of heat

lines leads or ropes with which dogs pull sleds

magnetic attracting iron or steel like a magnet

mammal warm-blooded, air-breathing animal with fur or hair

opaque material through which light cannot pass

ozone a gas in the atmosphere that absorbs some of the Sun's rays

snowmobile a vehicle with tracks and skis for traveling on snow

spiral a circular curve that gets wider and wider, like a snail's shell

ventilation allowing the passage of air

wilderness large area of wild, empty land

Further information

Books

Arctic 24 Hours by Lorrie Mack (Dorling Kindersley, 2007)
A day in the life of the Arctic, mainly looking at how creatures live there.

Arctic Peoples: What life was like in the most Northerly reaches of the Earth by Jen Green (Southwater, 2004)
The history of the region, including projects.

Arctic Tundra, Life at the North Pole by Salvatore Tocci (Franklin Watts, 2005)
A description of plants and animals in the area, plus details of some early explorers.

Explorers Wanted at the North Pole by Simon Chapman (Egmont, 2004)
Fact-based brief for a mission to find a missing Arctic expedition.

Journey into the Arctic by Bryan and Cherry Alexander (OUP, 2003)
A trip by sled, snowmobile and icebreaker ship.

Films

Arctic Tale directed by Adam Ravetch, Sarah Robertson (Paramount Classics, 2007)
The harsh world of the Arctic described through the lives of two mother animals—a walrus and a polar bear.

The Day After Tomorrow directed by Roland Emmerich (20th Century Fox, 2004)
An action movie based on the idea of a sudden ice age freezing up New York.

An Inconvenient Truth directed by Davis Guggenheim (Paramount Classics, 2006)
Documentary presented by former U.S. Vice President Al Gore setting out the dangers of global warming.

Web sites

www.arctic.noaa.gov
The USA's National Oceanic and Atmospheric Association provides information and pictures.

www.athropolis.com/links/arctic.htm
Links to many informative and entertaining websites.

www.bbc.co.uk/cbbc/wild/arctic/
Information, video diaries, and interactive illustrations.

www.uspermafrost.org/kids.shtml
A wealth of information from the United States Permafrost Association with maps and profiles of Arctic peoples.

Index